Georg GOLTERMANN

(1824 – 1898)

Concerto No. 4 for Cello and Orchestra, Op. 65
G Major / Sol majeur / G-Dur

Edited by
Josef Hofer

DOWANI International

Preface

Georg Goltermann's Concerto No. 4 for cello and orchestra in G Major, Op. 65, is one of the easiest of the eight solo concertos he wrote for this instrument. Drawing closely on famous predecessors, such as Robert Schumann's A minor Concerto, his piece captivates the listener with a rich vein of melody, an expansive and elegiac slow movement, and a wittily amusing *Allegro molto* as a finale. It does not require knowledge of thumb positions and is a perfect teaching piece for advanced learners.

The first CD (CD A) opens with the concert version of each movement (cello and orchestra). After tuning your instrument (Track 1 on both CDs), the musical work can begin. First, you will hear the piano accompaniment at slow tempo (CD A) and medium tempo (CD B) for practice purposes. At slow tempo you can also hear the cello played softly in the background as a guide. Having mastered these levels, you can now play the piece with orchestra at the original tempo (CD B). Each movement has been sensibly divided into subsections for practice purposes. You can select the subsection you want using the track numbers indicated in the solo part. Further explanations can be found at the end of this volume along with the names of the musicians involved in the recording. More detailed information can be found in the Internet at www.dowani.com. All of the versions were recorded live.

The fingering and bowing marks in this edition were provided by Josef Hofer, a cellist and teacher living in Liechtenstein. Hofer studied with Walter Grimmer in Berne and Gerhard Mantel in Frankfurt am Main. He is well known as a chamber musician and jury member at various national and international competitions and has taught for many years in Liechtenstein and Switzerland.

We wish you lots of fun playing from our *DOWANI 3 Tempi Play Along* editions and hope that your musicality and diligence will enable you to play the concert version as soon as possible. Our goal is to provide the essential conditions you need for effective practicing through motivation, enjoyment and fun.

Your DOWANI Team

Avant-propos

Georg Goltermann a composé huit concertos pour violoncelle et orchestre parmi lesquelles son concerto n° 4 op. 65 en Sol majeur est un des plus faciles sur le plan technique. Faisant référence à d'autres concertos pour violoncelle connus – comme par exemple le concerto en la mineur de Robert Schumann – ce concerto séduit par son style mélodique, son deuxième mouvement lent et étendu au caractère élégiaque ainsi que par son *Allegro molto* amusant et humoristique à la fin du morceau. Ce concerto peut être joué sans avoir appris les positions du pouce et il est approprié à l'enseignement des élèves avancés.

Le premier CD (CD A) vous permettra d'entendre d'abord la version de concert de chaque mouvement (violoncelle et orchestre). Après avoir accordé votre instrument (sur les deux CDs plage n° 1), vous pourrez commencer le travail musical. Pour travailler le morceau au tempo lent (CD A) et au tempo moyen (CD B), vous entendrez l'accompagnement de piano. Au tempo lent, le violoncelle restera cependant toujours audible très doucement à l'arrière-plan. Vous pourrez ensuite jouer le tempo original (CD B) avec accompagnement d'orchestre. Chaque mouvement a été divisé en sections judicieuses pour faciliter le travail.

Vous pouvez sélectionner ces sections à l'aide des numéros de plages indiqués dans la partie du soliste. Pour obtenir plus d'informations et les noms des artistes qui ont participé aux enregistrements, veuillez consulter la dernière page de cette édition ou notre site Internet : www.dowani.com. Toutes les versions ont été enregistrées en direct.

Les doigtés et indications des coups d'archet proviennent du violoncelliste et pédagogue Josef Hofer qui vit au Liechtenstein. Il étudia auprès de Walter Grimmer à Berne et Gerhard Mantel à Francfort-sur-le-Main. Josef Hofer est musicien de chambre et membre de jury de divers concours nationaux et internationaux. Il enseigne depuis de nombreuses années au Liechtenstein et en Suisse.

Nous vous souhaitons beaucoup de plaisir à faire de la musique avec la collection *DOWANI 3 Tempi Play Along* et nous espérons que votre musicalité et votre application vous amèneront aussi rapidement que possible à la version de concert. Notre but est de vous offrir les bases nécessaires pour un travail efficace par la motivation et le plaisir.

Les Éditions DOWANI

Vorwort

Das Konzert Nr. 4 für Cello und Orchester op. 65 in G-Dur von Georg Goltermann gehört zu den technisch leichtesten der insgesamt acht Solo-Konzerte, die er für dieses Instrument geschrieben hat. Ganz in Anlehnung an bekannte Cellokonzerte – wie das Konzert in a-moll von Robert Schumann – besticht dieses Konzert durch seine reiche Melodik, einen elegischen, weit ausholenden langsamen Satz und durch ein witzig humoristisches *Allegro molto* am Schluss. Das Konzert kann ohne Kenntnisse der Daumenlage gespielt werden und eignet sich hervorragend als Unterrichtsliteratur für fortgeschrittene Schüler.

Auf der ersten CD (CD A) können Sie zuerst die Konzertversion (Cello mit Orchester) eines jeden Satzes anhören. Nach dem Stimmen Ihres Instrumentes (auf beiden CDs Track 1) kann die musikalische Arbeit beginnen. Zum Üben folgt nun im langsamen (CD A) und mittleren Tempo (CD B) die Klavierbegleitung, wobei im langsamen Tempo das Cello als Orientierung leise im Hintergrund zu hören ist. Anschließend können Sie sich im Originaltempo (CD B) vom Orchester begleiten lassen. Jeder Satz wurde in sinnvolle Übe-Abschnitte unterteilt. Diese können Sie mit Hilfe der in der Solostimme angegebenen Track-Nummern auswählen. Weitere Erklärungen hierzu sowie die Namen der Künstler finden Sie auf der letzten Seite dieser Ausgabe; ausführlichere Informationen können Sie im Internet unter www.dowani.com nachlesen. Alle eingespielten Versionen wurden live aufgenommen.

Die Fingersätze und Striche in dieser Ausgabe stammen von dem in Liechtenstein lebenden Cellisten und Pädagogen Josef Hofer. Er studierte bei Walter Grimmer in Bern sowie bei Gerhard Mantel in Frankfurt am Main. Josef Hofer ist als Kammermusiker und Jurymitglied bei diversen nationalen und internationalen Wettbewerben tätig und unterrichtet seit vielen Jahren in Liechtenstein und der Schweiz.

Wir wünschen Ihnen viel Spaß beim Musizieren mit unseren *DOWANI 3 Tempi Play Along*-Ausgaben und hoffen, dass Ihre Musikalität und Ihr Fleiß Sie möglichst bald bis zur Konzertversion führen werden. Unser Ziel ist es, Ihnen durch Motivation, Freude und Spaß die notwendigen Voraussetzungen für effektives Üben zu schaffen.

Ihr DOWANI Team

Concerto No. 4

for Cello and Orchestra, Op. 65

G Major / Sol majeur / G-Dur

G. Goltermann (1824 – 1898)

DOW 3500

8

attacca:

Georg GOLTERMANN

(1824 – 1898)

Concerto No. 4 for Cello and Orchestra, Op. 65
G Major / Sol majeur / G-Dur

Cello / Violoncelle / Violoncello

DOWANI International

Cello

Concerto No. 4

for Cello and Orchestra, Op. 65
G Major / Sol majeur / G-Dur

I A2

G. Goltermann (1824 – 1898)
Edited by J. Hofer

DOW 3500

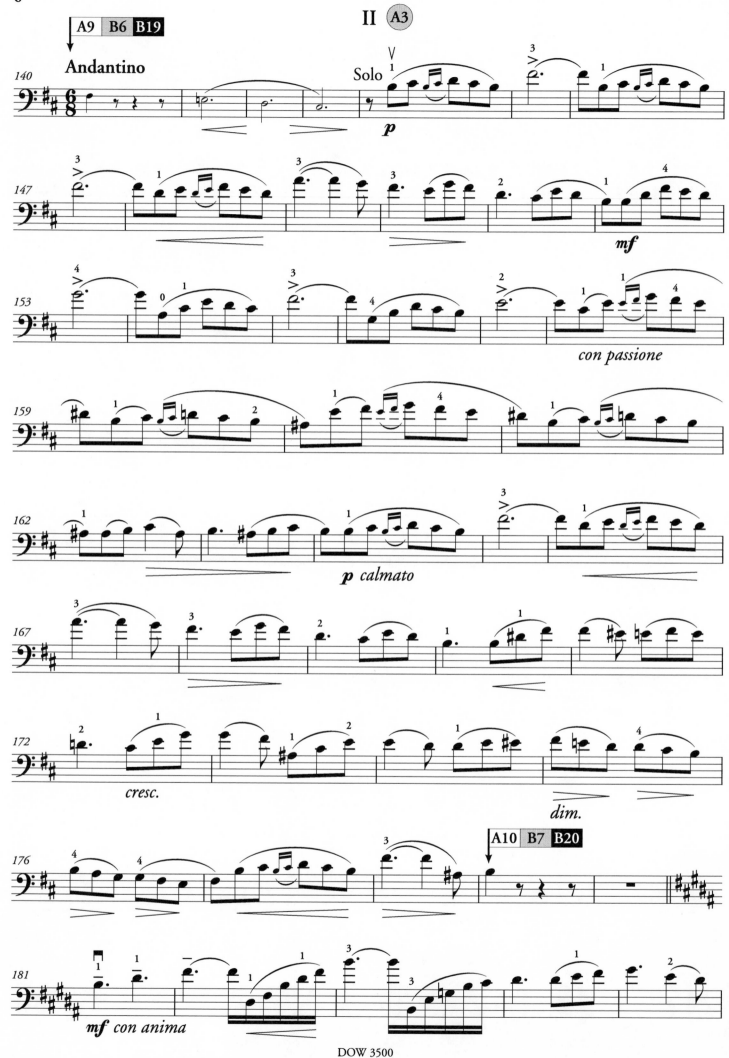

12

16

ENGLISH

DOWANI CD:

- Track No. 1

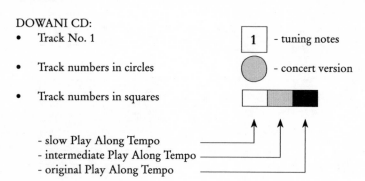

| 1 | - tuning notes |

- Track numbers in circles — ● - concert version

- Track numbers in squares — ▭ (white/grey/black bar)

- slow Play Along Tempo
- intermediate Play Along Tempo
- original Play Along Tempo

- Additional tracks for longer movements or pieces
- **Double CD:** CD1 = A, CD2 = B
- **Concert version:** cello and orchestra
- **Slow tempo:** piano accompaniment with cello in the background
- **Intermediate tempo:** piano accompaniment only
- **Original tempo:** orchestra only

Please note that the recorded version of the piano accompaniment may diff
slightly from the sheet music. This is due to the spontaneous character of li
music making and the artistic freedom of the musicians. The original sheet
music for the solo part is, of course, not affected.

FRANÇAIS

DOWANI CD:

- Plage N° 1

| 1 | - diapason |

- N° de plage dans un cercle — ● - version de concert

- N° de plage dans un rectangle — ▭ (white/grey/black bar)

- tempo lent play along
- tempo moyen play along
- tempo original play along

- Plages supplémentaires pour mouvements ou morceaux longs
- **Double CD:** CD1 = A, CD2 = B
- **Version de concert :** violoncelle et orchestre
- **Tempo lent :** accompagnement de piano avec violoncelle en fond sonore
- **Tempo moyen :** seulement l'accompagnement de piano
- **Tempo original :** seulement l'accompagnement d'orchestre

L'enregistrement de l'accompagnement de piano peut présenter quelques
différences mineures par rapport au texte de la partition. Ceci est du à la liberté
artistique des musiciens et résulte d'un jeu spontané et vivant, mais n'affecte,
bien entendu, d'aucune manière la partie soliste.

DEUTSCH

DOWANI CD:

- Track Nr. 1

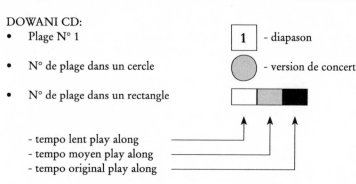

| 1 | - Stimmtöne |

- Trackangabe im Kreis — ● - Konzertversion

- Trackangabe im Rechteck — ▭ (white/grey/black bar)

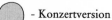

- langsames Play Along Tempo
- mittleres Play Along Tempo
- originales Play Along Tempo

- Zusätzliche Tracks bei längeren Sätzen oder Stücken
- **Doppel-CD:** CD1 = A, CD2 = B
- **Konzertversion:** Violoncello und Orchester
- **Langsames Tempo:** Klavierbegleitung mit Violoncello im Hintergrund
- **Mittleres Tempo:** nur Klavierbegleitung
- **Originaltempo:** nur Orchester

Die Klavierbegleitung auf der CD-Aufnahme kann gegenüber dem Notente
kleine Abweichungen aufweisen. Dies geht in der Regel auf die künstlerisch
Freiheit der Musiker und auf spontanes, lebendiges Musizieren zurück. Die
Solostimme bleibt davon selbstverständlich unangetastet.

DOWANI - 3 Tempi Play Along is published by:
DOWANI International
A division of De Haske (International) AG
Postfach 60, CH-6332 Hagendorn
Switzerland
Phone: +41-(0)41-785 82 50 / Fax +41-(0)41-785 82 58
Email: info@dowani.com
www.dowani.com

Recording & Digital Mastering: Pavel Lavrenenkov, Russia
Music Notation: Notensatz Thomas Metzinger, Germany
Design: Andreas Haselwanter, Austria

Concert Versio
Sergey Sudzilovsky, Cell
Russian Philharmonic Orchestra Moscov
Konstantin Krimets, Conducto

3 Tempi Accompanimen
Slow
Vitaly Junitsky, Pian

Intermediat
Vitaly Junitsky, Pian

Origina
Russian Philharmonic Orchestra Moscov
Konstantin Krimets, Conducto